W9-AFS-748

Isaac Asimov's
21st Century
Library of the
Universe

Near and Far

Black Holes, Pulsars, and Quasars

BY ISAAC ASIMOV
WITH REVISIONS AND UPDATING BY RICHARD HANTULA

Gareth Stevens Publishing
A WORLD ALMANAC EDUCATION GROUP COMPANY

Please visit our web site at: **www.garethstevens.com**
For a free color catalog describing Gareth Stevens Publishing's list of high-quality books and multimedia programs, call 1-800-542-2595 (USA) or 1-800-387-3178 (Canada). Gareth Stevens Publishing's fax: (414) 332-3567.

Library of Congress Cataloging-in-Publication Data

Asimov, Isaac.
    Black holes, pulsars, and quasars / by Isaac Asimov; with revisions and updating by Richard Hantula.
        p. cm. — (Isaac Asimov's 21st century library of the universe. Near and far)
    Includes bibliographical references and index.
    ISBN 0-8368-3965-X (lib. bdg.)
    1. Cosmology—Juvenile literature. 2. Astronomy—Juvenile literature. 3. Stars—Juvenile literature. 4. Black holes (Astronomy)—Juvenile literature. I. Hantula, Richard. II. Asimov, Isaac. Mysteries of deep space. III. Title.
    QB983.A864   2005
    523.8—dc22   2004058939

This edition first published in 2005 by
Gareth Stevens Publishing
A WRC Media Company
330 West Olive Street, Suite 100
Milwaukee, WI 53212 USA

Series editor: Mark J. Sachner
Cover design and layout adaptation: Melissa Valuch
Picture research: Kathy Keller
Additional picture research: Diane Laska-Swanke
Artwork commissioning: Kathy Keller and Laurie Shock
Production director: Jessica Morris

The editors at Gareth Stevens Publishing have selected science author Richard Hantula to bring this classic series of young people's information books up to date. Richard Hantula has written and edited books and articles on science and technology for more than two decades. He was the senior U.S. editor for the *Macmillan Encyclopedia of Science.*

In addition to Hantula's contribution to this most recent edition, the editors would like to acknowledge the participation of two noted science authors, Greg Walz-Chojnacki and Francis Reddy, as contributors to earlier editions of this work.

Contents

We live in an enormously large place – the Universe. It's only natural that we would want to understand this place, so scientists and engineers have developed instruments and spacecraft that have told us far more about the Universe than we could possibly imagine.

We have seen planets up close, and spacecraft have even landed on some. We have learned about colliding galaxies and dark matter. We have gathered amazing data about how the Universe may have come into being and how it may end. Nothing could be more astonishing.

We have learned new things about the stars, too. People at one time thought of the Universe as a quiet place. The stars seemed serene and unchanging. Now we know that a huge star can explode and then collapse into a tiny tightly packed body called a neutron star that can do incredible things. Neutron stars known as pulsars give off rapid pulses of electromagnetic radiation such as radio waves. We know that galaxies can have incredibly active centers, called quasars, and that there are black holes in space. Nothing that falls into a black hole can escape!

Unruly Stars

In the beginning, after the Big Bang, the Universe became filled with large clouds of dust and gas. Some of these clouds began to contract under their own gravitational pull. In each of these clouds, the matter packed together and increased in temperature. Finally, if the matter became packed enough and hot enough, it developed into a star, perhaps accompanied by planets. Our Sun formed this way nearly five billion years ago.

Stars and planets still form out of clouds of dust and gas. One such cloud is the Orion Nebula, where astronomers can see small, dark, round spots. These are collapsing clouds that will eventually become shining stars with, possibly, planets.

Stars do not stay still. And they do not always behave themselves! Some twinkle, and some explode. Some collapse, and some collide with other stars. With its billions upon billions of stars, it is no wonder our Universe is such a fascinating place.

Right, top: The birth of the Sun began with the collapse of a cloud of gas and dust (*upper left*). As the cloud contracted, the outer regions flattened into a disk (*center*). The cloud's center erupted in a blaze, and the Sun was born (*right*).

Right, bottom: A spectacular cloud of gases surrounds several hot stars deep inside the Orion Nebula. This cloud is visible to the naked eye as the middle star in the sword of the constellation Orion.

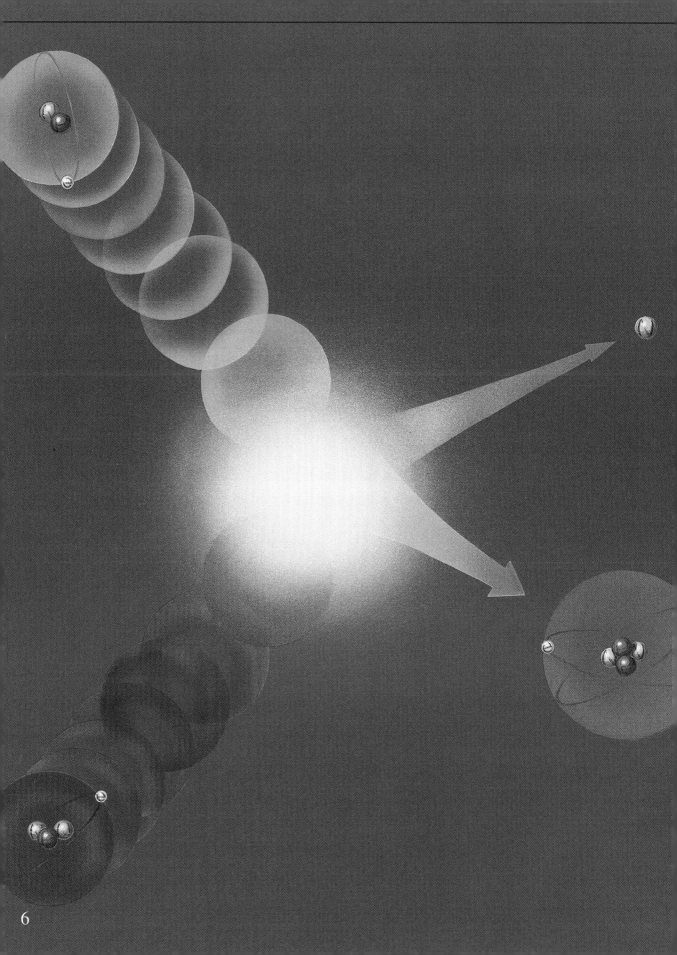

Shining Stars

Stars come in all sizes. Some are larger and brighter than the Sun. Most are smaller and dimmer. When stars form, they are made mostly of hydrogen, the lightest element. Tiny particles of hydrogen smash together and produce larger particles that make up the second lightest element, helium. This collision releases energy that keeps the stars shining.

This energy also keeps stars from collapsing under their own gravitational pull. Large stars have more hydrogen to begin with, but their centers are hotter than the centers of small stars. So large stars burn their hydrogen more quickly than small stars.

Left: This illustration shows how fusion of hydrogen into helium might be performed on Earth to create energy. Two atoms of hydrogen in the form of deuterium *(upper left)* and tritium *(lower left)* actually have a bit more mass than the helium *(lower right)* and neutron *(upper right)* that are made by this process. The difference represents the energy released. Another form of fusion produces helium in the Sun to create sunshine.

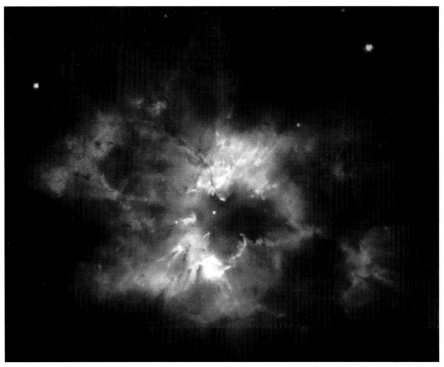

Above: The dot at the center of this picture is a hot, tiny white dwarf star in our Galaxy, the Milky Way. It was formed when a red giant star collapsed, throwing out a massive cloud of gas – called a planetary nebula – which can now be seen around the star.

Above: A black hole. What remains of a star after it explodes can be so dense that it imprisons even its own light. Although it may be called a hole, it is really an object of great mass. This illustration shows how the immense gravity of the dead star creates a deep well from which nothing can escape.

As a star continues to shine, its center grows steadily hotter, and its hydrogen runs low. The extra heat makes it expand. Because of this expansion, the outer layers change to a cool red. The result is a red giant or even a supergiant. As the big red star continues to shine, it finally runs out of energy at its center. Then it collapses.

In the case of extremely large stars, this collapse is so rapid and violent that it creates an enormous explosion – a supernova. For a brief while the supernova shines as brightly in the sky as an entire galaxy ordinarily does.

After such an explosion, some matter flies into space and some remains behind. The matter that remains behind will become a neutron star or, if the original star was particularly massive, a black hole.

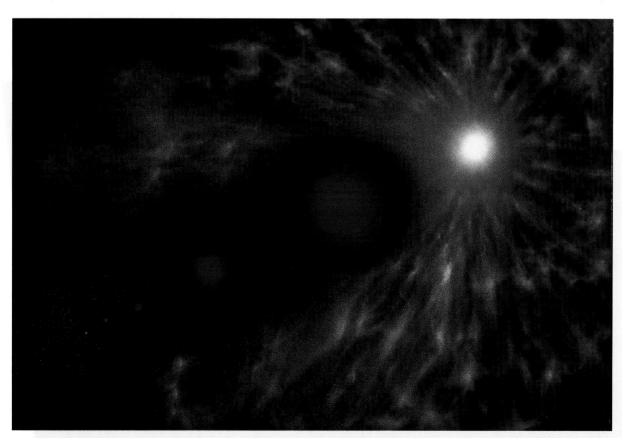

Above: From star to supernova – going out in a blaze of glory!

Small, but Mighty – The White Dwarf

When an ordinary star like the Sun collapses, a bit of its mass is thrown out into space. What remains is squeezed down by gravity to the size of a small planet. The result is a tiny star called a white dwarf. If the mass of the Sun were squeezed into a white dwarf the size of Earth or less, a bit of the white-dwarf matter about the size of your little finger would weigh at least 20 tons. If the star is larger than the Sun to begin with, its greater gravity forces it together even more tightly. It becomes a neutron star, with all the mass of an ordinary star squeezed into a little ball perhaps 12 miles (20 km) across. Or if the original star was extremely large, it turns into a black hole.

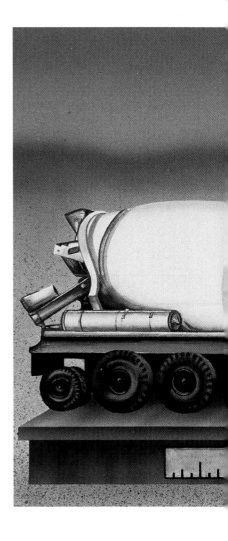

A neutron star — small matter, lots of mass!

Our Sun is too small to collapse into a neutron star. But what if it could? All its mass would be squeezed into a ball that might be only 8 miles (13 km) across. The neutron star would take up only one-quadrillionth the space the Sun did. But a piece of its matter would weigh a quadrillion (1,000,000,000,000,000) times more than the same size piece of matter from the Sun. Suppose you made a ballpoint pen out of neutron star matter. A pen made of ordinary matter might weigh half an ounce (14 grams). But a pen that was made of neutron star matter would weigh 15 billion tons!

This illustration gives you an idea of what happens when a star collapses into a white dwarf or a neutron star. Imagine a 20-ton cement mixer turning into a cement mixer the size of your little finger and still weighing 20 tons!

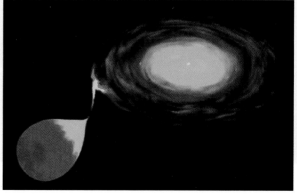

Above: These two drawings illustrate binary ("double") star systems in which a star (shown on the right in each of the pictures) has collapsed into itself by the force of its own gravity and become so dense that it is siphoning off matter from its stellar neighbor. As the matter circles the collapsed star, it swirls into an accretion disk. Some neutron stars are so densely packed, the force of their gravity so powerful, that they can only be identified by observing their accretion disks.

Celestial Energy

In 1054, Chinese, Arab, and American Indian sky watchers looked up to the heavens and saw the result of a supernova that had exploded 6,500 light-years away from them. (One light-year is how far light travels in one year.) This supernova formed a huge, expanding cloud of dust and gas that we can still see. The cloud is called the Crab Nebula. At its center is a tiny neutron star, all that is left of the exploded star.

This neutron star turns thirty times a second, sending a pulse of energy toward Earth with each turn. This energy is in the form of electromagnetic waves called radio waves. Scientists first noticed these pulses in the Crab Nebula in 1968 and began calling such neutron stars *pulsars*. The Crab pulsar also sends out pulses of other types of radiation — such as light and X rays — thirty times a second.

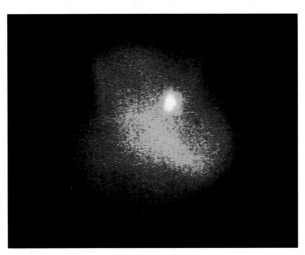

Left: The hot inner regions of the Crab Nebula. The bright spot is the Crab pulsar. In one second, it blinks on and off thirty times. It is pictured here with its light on.

Stars speaking from space!

Radio waves that flickered, or twinkled, rapidly from the sky were first detected in 1967 by a British astronomy student named Jocelyn Bell. For a while some people wondered if these waves were signals from beings in space. Scientists called them LGM, for Little Green Men. But the twinkles were so regular that scientists decided they couldn't be of intelligent origin. It turned out that Bell had discovered pulsars — spinning neutron stars that send out radio waves with each turn they make.

In 1054, astronomers saw a supernova, the Crab Nebula, whose "ashes" we see today as a cloud of hot gas. Today's technology can photograph the cloud to reveal its chemical parts. This photo shows the presence of hydrogen (red) and sulfur (blue) in the nebula.

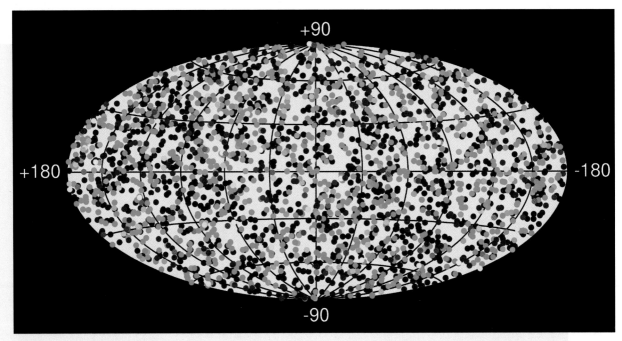

Above: Gamma-ray bursts can occur anywhere in the sky, as shown by this map of bursts detected over several years by the *Compton Gamma-Ray Observatory* spacecraft. Our Milky Way Galaxy lies along the line running horizontally across the middle of the map.

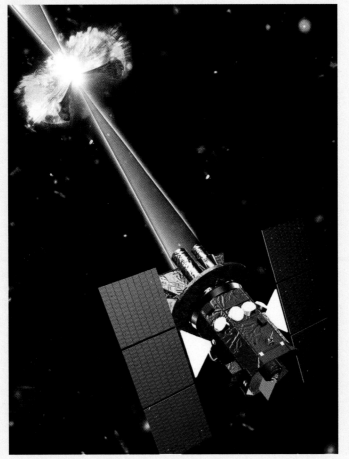

Left: An artist's conception of a satellite, scheduled to be launched into Earth orbit in 2005, whose mission will be to monitor gamma ray "bursts" coming from space. In this illustration, the bursts are emanating from a supermassive black hole.

Mystery Bursts

In the 1960s and 1970s artificial satellites orbiting Earth detected "bursts" of gamma rays coming from space. Gamma rays are a type of electromagnetic radiation that is even more energetic than X rays. The most powerful of such bursts pack into a brief flash as much energy as the output of several galaxies. The bursts had not been detected from the ground before artificial satellites came into use, because gamma rays cannot pass through Earth's atmosphere.

As more and more bursts were observed, it became clear that they occurred over the entire sky, not just in the region of our Galaxy, the Milky Way. This meant the bursters, as the unknown sources of the bursts were called, were probably located in other galaxies. By the late 1990s scientists began to succeed in measuring the distances of some bursters from Earth. It turned out that they were billions of light-years away!

Some bursts last for less than two seconds; others — "long-duration bursts" — last a little longer. Some astronomers think long-duration bursts may be caused by a special kind of supernova that gives birth to a black hole. But even if supernovas can account for all long-duration gamma-ray bursts, that leaves the cause of short-duration ones still unknown.

Pulsars — you can set your watch by them.

Pulsars turn so steadily in the sky that they could be used as nearly perfect clocks. In fact, pulsars have been used to chart Earth's position in the Galaxy. On board the *Pioneer 10* and *11* space probes are plaques containing information about the location of Earth. Pulsars are included in maps on these plaques. Scientists know that the rates at which these pulsars turn would change very little in the time it might take for the plaques to be discovered by other beings in space — perhaps millions of years. So these maps would help extraterrestrial beings locate Earth from anywhere in the Galaxy.

A Matter of Gravity

We know that gravity is a force that attracts objects to one another. But can you imagine what gravity actually looks like? Picture gravity by pretending space is a rubber sheet. Any heavy object resting on the sheet puts a dent in it. The heavier the object, the deeper the dent. If an object is kept heavy but is made smaller, the weight is concentrated on a smaller area, and the dent gets deeper. A white dwarf makes a much deeper dent than Earth does. A neutron star makes a still deeper dent. The deeper the dent, the harder it would be for an object to escape if it fell in. What if something were so small and heavy that it formed a dent too deep for anything to escape – ever? That something would be a black hole.

Right, opposite: This diagram shows the pull of the gravitational fields of three objects: *(left to right)* the Sun, a neutron star, and a black hole. See how the large Sun barely distorts the grid. The smaller neutron star distorts the grid somewhat with its more concentrated mass. The smallest object – the black hole – distorts the grid lines most of all due to its tremendous gravitational pull.

Double pulsars – a recipe for trouble?

Astronomers have found cases where two pulsars are close and circling each other. All the while, they are giving off radiation and losing energy. This causes them to get slightly closer to each other with every turn. Eventually, they will collide. What will happen when two pulsars collide? The mass will double. The mass might grow so large that the resulting increased gravity will cause it to collapse into a black hole.

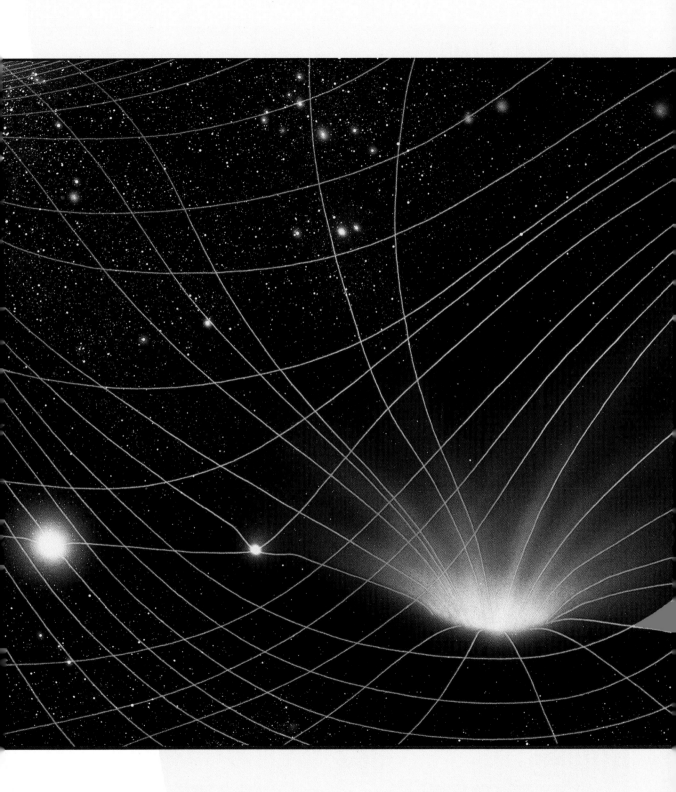

Black holes do not permit even light to escape — which means they cannot be seen. But then how is it possible to find them? Scientists try to identify a black hole through its interactions with matter that they can detect.

If the black hole orbits a star, for example, some of the star's gas may flow into the black hole. As gas falls toward the hole, it swirls into a flattened disk. Its molecules move ever faster, bunching up and colliding. This makes the gas very hot — so hot that it gives off X rays! Although we can't see the black hole, satellites can detect X rays.

Scientists think an enormous, "supermassive" black hole lies at the heart of many galaxies. They find signs of the existence of such black holes by observing material swirling around and shooting out of the region surrounding the galaxy core. Their research may involve observations made with X rays, light, and other types of electromagnetic radiation, such as radio waves.

Opposite: The small, flat, spiral disk (*upper right*) shows that a black hole is stealing matter from its neighboring star. X rays given off by the whirling matter tell us a black hole exists here, although the black hole itself is invisible.

Mini-black holes: a mega-problem?

According to British scientist Stephen Hawking, black holes can slowly "evaporate." The smaller they are, the more quickly they evaporate, finally disappearing in an explosion. Known black holes are probably too large to show noticeable evaporation. But it is possible that there may exist mini-black holes, having about the same mass as an asteroid, whose lifetime would be relatively "short." Such miniature black holes might be scattered through space but could be detected only when they are close to Earth. What would happen to Earth if a mini-black hole approached our Solar System? Scientists do not know.

A Black Hole Reality

Astronomers have detected a great deal of energy coming from the centers of many galaxies. For a long time, scientists thought there were enormous black holes lying in the middle of these galaxies. The first solid evidence for the existence of such a black hole came in 1994 from astronomers who were using the Hubble Space Telescope to look at the center of the giant galaxy M87. This galaxy lies in the constellation Virgo and is located about 50 million light-years from Earth. In the core of the galaxy, astronomers found signs of an extremely powerful black hole. This black hole appeared to have as much mass as up to three billion Suns, yet it occupied less space than our Solar System!

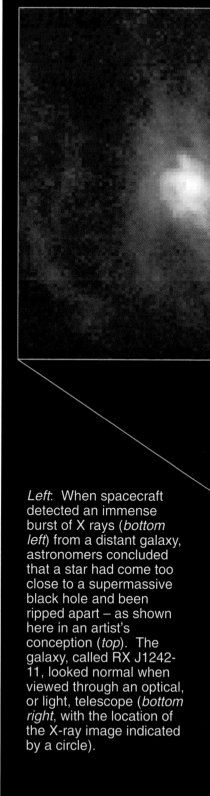

Left: When spacecraft detected an immense burst of X rays (*bottom left*) from a distant galaxy, astronomers concluded that a star had come too close to a supermassive black hole and been ripped apart – as shown here in an artist's conception (*top*). The galaxy, called RX J1242-11, looked normal when viewed through an optical, or light, telescope (*bottom right*, with the location of the X-ray image indicated by a circle).

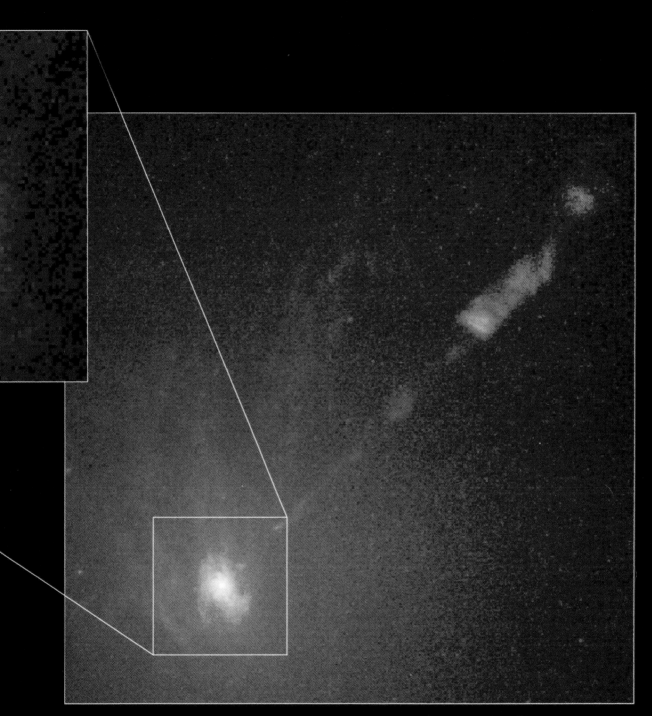

M87 is a galaxy with an enormous "jet" of material shooting from its heart. The
Hubble Space Telescope was able to peer into the galaxy's heart and see a disk
(inset). Measurements of the disk showed it was spinning at a rate of over 1 million
miles (1.6 million km) per hour. Only the gravity of a black hole could keep such
speedy material in orbit. Scientists found that the black hole may weigh as much as
three billion Suns but is concentrated into a space smaller than our Solar System.

The Bright Light of Quasars

The Universe is full of objects that fascinate and puzzle us. In the past, one such group of objects looked like faint stars. At first, astronomers thought these objects were ordinary stars of our own Galaxy — except that they gave off radio waves. But then astronomers watched them more closely and studied their light. By 1963, it was determined that these objects lay outside the Milky Way, up to several billion light-years away.

The objects were called *quasi-stellar radio sources* — *quasars* for short. Astronomers soon found additional distant "quasi-stellar" (or "starlike") objects, many of which were not radio sources. These quasi-stellar objects lie in galaxies at distances of 800 million light-years to more than 12 billion light-years from Earth. These galaxies are so far away that they wouldn't normally be seen, except for the fact that their centers are unusually luminous — they give off so much energy they are up to hundreds or even thousands of times more luminous than the entire Milky Way. It is these extra-bright centers that are quasars. Scientists think that the extreme brightness of a quasar is connected with the presence of a supermassive black hole at the galaxy center. Such a black hole could draw in all sorts of glowing matter, from stars to dust.

Left: A quasar *(bottom)* interacts with a nearby galaxy, drawing in matter to the quasar's center.

If we could see to the edge
of the Universe, might we
find newly formed galaxies,
like this spiral, with a quasar
as its center?

The redshift at a glance. A galaxy's hydrogen atoms can emit blue light, as seen in the galaxy pictured *(on the left)*. However, that same light will appear redder and redder *(on the right)* as we look at galaxies located farther from Earth. The colors of the spectrum *(bottom)* also show a greater shift toward the red end of the spectrum as the galaxies move farther away from Earth.

The Redshift

How can we tell that quasars and gamma-ray bursters are so far away? Because certain scientific instruments can spread the light from an object into a "spectrum," or rainbow, of colors — red, orange, yellow, green, blue, indigo, and violet. Dark lines cross this rainbow. When an object that gives off light moves away from Earth, they move, or shift, toward the red end of the spectrum. The faster the object travels, the farther the shift toward red. Since the Universe is expanding, distant objects are all moving away and show this redshift. The greater the redshift, the farther away they are.

When quasars were discovered, their great redshifts led scientists to view them as the farthest known objects in the Universe. But scientists later observed gamma-ray bursts with redshifts also indicating distances of billions of light-years from Earth.

Quasars and bursters give off enormous amounts of energy, but it is sometimes possible to detect other extremely remote objects that are not so luminous. If a large object such as a galaxy cluster happens to lie between the remote object and Earth, its powerful gravity may act like a lens, amplifying light from the remote object. In this way, scientists have detected dim galaxies that, according to their redshifts, are more than 13 billion light-years from Earth.

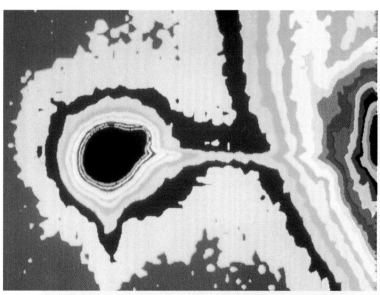

Above: In this computer-enhanced image, a quasar *(left)* seems to be interacting with a galaxy *(right)*. The big question: Are the two really attached? Most astronomers believe the quasar is actually many times farther away from us than the galaxy.

Was Our Galaxy Once a Quasar?

When we see a quasar that is 12 billion light-years away, we know that the light from this quasar took 12 billion years to reach Earth. This means we see the quasar as it was 12 billion years ago. This would be when it and the Universe — which we think is 13.7 billion years old — were very young. So the fact that quasars are so far away may mean that young galaxies — which shine very brightly — are more likely to be quasars than old ones. Perhaps our own Milky Way Galaxy was a quasar billions of years ago, but then it settled down. If so, that's a good thing. A galactic center burning as brightly as a quasar would fill the galaxy with so much energy that it might not be possible for life to develop in it.

Left: An X-ray view of the center of our Milky Way Galaxy, from the *Chandra X-Ray Observatory* spacecraft. Astronomers believe a supermassive black hole lies at the middle of the picture. A jet of material can be faintly seen shooting toward the *lower left*.

A close encounter of the galactic kind!

Our Milky Way and the Andromeda Galaxy lie in the same cluster. Some scientists expect them to collide in a few billion years. Imagine these two colossal star systems — each containing hundreds of billions of stars — smacking into each other! However, there is a great deal of room between the stars in each galaxy and few, if any, stars would actually collide. The galaxies would probably slide through each other. But they would be shaken by gravity, and our own Sun could go spinning off, leaving its home galaxy forever. But don't worry just yet — it won't happen until a long time from now!

Above: The Milky Way and the Andromeda Galaxy – will they collide? Or will they just slide through each other? Evidence suggests that our neighboring galaxy may have already swallowed up a smaller galaxy.

Fact File: Quasar, the Prize for Power

What we can see of quasars comes to us from distances so vast that we can barely imagine how far away, and how long ago, they existed. Quasars may be outshined by the most powerful gamma-ray bursters. But the gamma-ray bursts are short flashes of energy. Quasars pump out power continuously, and in this sense can lay claim to the title of the sky's most powerful energy source.

On these pages are two pictures. Picture A is of a spiral galaxy with a quasar at its core. Picture B gives a close-up look at the core, showing the black hole that may lie at the heart of the quasar.

Picture A

Subject:

• A violent spiral galaxy deep in the cosmos.

Special Features:

• High-energy quasar at galactic core.

• Black hole at center.

• Accretion disk — a gravitational whirlpool of hot gas in a ring around the center feeding the black hole and the quasar.

• Gas jets spewing particles at right angles to disk.

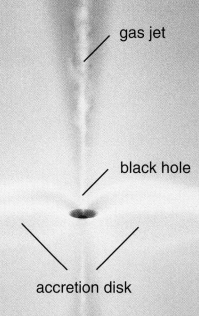

B

gas jet

black hole

accretion disk

Picture B

Subject:

• A detailed view of the galactic core, showing the quasar and its black hole center.

Special Features:

• Sideways view of accretion disk. The disk might stretch out to a diameter one hundred times that of our Solar System.

• Black hole at center of disk. Because of the enormous amount of stellar matter that is swirling around the center, the black hole would not normally be visible. A black hole like this might have the mass of billions of stars the size of our Sun jammed into a space that is smaller than our Solar System.

• Jets shooting matter at a right angle to the accretion disk. The matter shoots out to distances that could approach millions of light-years. This would be farther than the distance between our Milky Way and its nearest galactic neighbor, the Andromeda Galaxy.

More Books about Black Holes, Pulsars, and Quasars

Black Holes. Don Nardo (Lucent)

The Life and Death of Stars. Ray Spangenburg and Kit Moser (Franklin Watts)

The Mystery of Black Holes. Chris Oxlade (Sagebrush Bound)

Smithsonian Intimate Guide to the Cosmos. Dana Berry (Smithsonian)

Sun and Stars. Barrett (Franklin Watts)

DVDs

The Expanding Universe. (Image Entertainment)

Stargaze II - Visions of the Universe (Wea)

Stephen Hawking's Universe. (Paramount Home Video)

Web Sites

The Internet is a good place to get more information about black holes, pulsars, quasars, and other celestial objects. The web sites listed here can help you learn about the most recent discoveries, as well as those made in the past.

Falling into a Black Hole. casa.colorado.edu/~ajsh/schw.shtml

Jodrell Bank Pulsar Group. www.jb.man.ac.uk/~pulsar/

NASA, Imagine the Universe Science. imagine.gsfc.nasa.gov/docs/science/science.html

Students for the Exploration and Development of Space. seds.lpl.arizona.edu/messier/

Windows to the Universe. www.windows.ucar.edu/tour/link=/the_universe/the_universe.html

Places to Visit

Here are some museums and planetariums where you can find a variety of exhibits and shows about black holes, pulsars, quasars, and other celestial objects.

**Adler Planetarium and
 Astronomy Museum**
1300 S. Lake Shore Drive
Chicago, IL 60605-2403

American Museum of Natural History
Rose Center for Earth and Space
Central Park West at 79th Street
New York, NY 10024

Montreal Planetarium
1000, rue Saint-Jacques Ouest
Montréal (Québec) H3C 1G7
Canada

Museum of Science, Boston
Science Park
Boston, MA 02114

National Air and Space Museum
Smithsonian Institution
6th and Independence Avenue SW
Washington, DC 20560

Scienceworks Museum
2 Booker Street
Spotswood
Melbourne, Victoria 3015
Australia

Glossary

Big Bang: a huge explosion that scientists think created our Universe about 13.7 billion years ago.

black hole: a tightly packed object with such powerful gravity that not even light can escape from it.

constellation: a grouping of stars in the sky that seems to trace out a familiar pattern, figure, or symbol.

electromagnetic radiation: such forms of radiation as gamma rays, X rays, ultraviolet radiation, light, infrared radiation, radio waves, and microwaves.

fusion: the smashing together of highly heated atoms to create larger atoms, such as the fusion of hydrogen atoms to produce helium atoms. The process can release huge amounts of energy.

galaxy: a large star system containing up to hundreds of billions of stars, along with gas and dust. Our Galaxy is known as the Milky Way.

gamma-ray burster: a distant object in another galaxy that releases a brief but intense flash in the form of electromagnetic radiation known as gamma rays.

gravity: the force that causes objects like Earth and the Moon to be drawn to one another.

helium: a light, colorless gas found in every star.

hydrogen: a colorless, odorless gas that is the simplest and lightest of the elements. Most stars are originally composed largely of hydrogen.

jet: a stream of fast-moving gas or similar material coming from the vicinity of an object such as a star or a black hole.

light-year: the distance light travels in one year - nearly 6 trillion miles (9.5 trillion km).

luminous: producing electromagnetic radiation, such as light.

Milky Way: the name of our Galaxy.

NASA: the space agency in the United States - the National Aeronautics and Space Administration.

neutron star: a star that has as much mass as an ordinary large star, but the mass — consisting mainly of the nuclear particles called neutrons — is squeezed into a much smaller ball.

pulsar: a rapidly rotating neutron star that sends out regular pulses of light, radio waves, or other electromagnetic waves.

quasar: an extremely distant object that seems to resemble a star and gives off huge amounts of energy. Quasars appear to be located at the centers of galaxies, and their activity involves an enormous black hole.

red giant: a large bright star that represents a late stage in the life of a star like our Sun, when its hydrogen fuel has run low and the star has expanded, with its outer layers becoming a cooler red.

redshift: the apparent reddening of the light given off by an object moving away from us. The greater the redshift of light from a distant galaxy, the farther away the galaxy is located and the faster it is moving away from us.

supernova: the explosive collapse of a very large star, which ends up as a neutron star or black hole.

white dwarf star: the small star that remains when a star uses up its store of nuclear fuel and collapses but does not explode.

Index

Born in 1920, Isaac Asimov came to the United States as a young boy from his native Russia. As a young man, he was a student of biochemistry. In time, he became one of the most productive writers the world has ever known. His books cover a spectrum of topics, including science, history, language theory, fantasy, and science fiction. His brilliant imagination gained him the respect and admiration of adults and children alike. Sadly, Isaac Asimov died shortly after the publication of the first edition of *Isaac Asimov's Library of the Universe.*

The publishers wish to thank the following for permission to reproduce copyright material: front cover, 3, 4-5 (lower), 8 (lower), 9, 18, 23, 29, © Mark Paternostro 1988; 4-5 (upper), 22, 25, National Optical Astronomy Observatories; 6-7, © Sally Bensusen 1987; 8 (upper), 11 (left), NASA Goddard Space Flight Center; 10-11 (upper), © Lynette Cook 1988; 11 (right), STScI, NASA; 12, Smithsonian Institution; 13, The Crab Nebula, Messier 1, From plates of the Hale 5m telescope, © Malin/Pasachoff/Caltech 1992; 14 (both), NASA; 17, © Julian Baum 1988; 20 (upper), NASA/CXC/M. Weiss; 20 (lower left), NASA/CXC/MPE/S. Komossa et al.; 20 (lower right), ESO/MPE/S. Komossa; 20-21, Holland Ford/NASA; 24, © Adolf Schaller 1988; 26, NASA/CXC/MIT/F.K. Baganoff et al.; 27, © Mark Paternostro 1983; 28, © Michael Carroll 1987.

FEB 1 6 2006